HAND-HELD EXECUTIONS

Paper: ISBN: 0-615-12311-2
First Edition

Publication by Del Sol Press/Web del Sol Association, a not-for-profit corporation under section 501 (c) (3) of the United States Internal Revenue Code.

The author gratefully acknowledges the editors of the following publications, in which some of the poems herein first appeared, some in slightly different form: *Black Warrior Review*: "Will is Leaving," "Winfred Arriving at Heaven's Lobby," "Winifred is Listening"; *Caffeine Destiny*: "Constructing Easter," "Nothing Sweet"; *Die Cast Garden*: Fundamental Vodoo"; *The Gettysburg Review*: "The Garden of Slow Demise"; *Harvard Review*: "Insomniac."

All essays herein first appeared in *The Boston Comment*, Web del Sol (webdelsol.com).

Cover Photo: Marek Uliasz

HAND-HELD EXECUTIONS

POEMS & ESSAYS

JOAN HOULIHAN

Del Sol Press ~ Washington, D.C. ~ 2003

Poems

I

II

III

IV

Essays

I

Biological Imperative

The wings suffer most. They stop shining.
A tilt of a nest, a backyard birch
black-sutured, half-dying—for this

we are bound to prepare. I am arrowed to you,
as if born of you, infrared in my bed of slosh
and song. The trajectory of us

can't be stopped. All the dead hum backwards
in the pretty spiral arm of their home.
Degradation: the white of their passing on.

H. Antecessor

All halted elegance, you make a paper wolf for me
then blow into a bottle for the howl. We are so merry
in the belly of July, knees pressed together, kissing

as we eat, while west, in Gran Dolina, the intact
skeletons are spread with tools around a cold hearth.
Trouble yourself: they are deformed

by a hammering for marrow along the longer
bones, and on the templar, blackened.
When man is a study of cut mark and fracture,

woman should be wary. I am not. Cloud-tails float
high, uncombed, as I, with found weed braided
simply in my hair, lean to your mouth.

Navigating February

From cataract and draped sheet, partially waked,
you grip down a wrought-iron rail, foot-blind.
The end of a season combines with harmful matter:
calomel of browned ice and salt.

You fell here once.
It wasn't your fault.

Deceptive melts expose slick spots,
ice-scored rind of fresh rock, all that ice abandons
in its retreat. Tuck your hand under my arm.

Some persistent failure,
a collapse of cold land formed us.
I could draw you a map,
all the proper boundaries intact.
Be careful.
The way is fracted and you, hard-breathing.

Take your time.
Each new fall makes it harder to rise.

As Winter Will

Mown, or lifted to the loft, our Summer hay
As on the lawn you were somber and said your lines:
Give the man a touch.
In need, your face looked upward,
Broke to mawkish, and a melancholy
Took your throat, the hope of a new alphabet,

Away. As winter will, it built spun-sugar
Crannies, and we crept, and prayed, took every care
Until your hair was topped with silver, my cheeks
So cold from your wise breath. I broke the frozen roses
And this was as close as we could get, and this
Was how we lived: in a drift of memory, a tilt toward
Youth. As if we could. As if now
Were not enough, in its clang, in its hand-
Held bell, in its taste of nickel, sharp.
In this fashion, our years flowed
And we made our bed with mortality, left the gates
Open, the mind vacant, intentionally.

I have given up everything. Nothing is
Left for you to pierce, examine; my youth
Is a small crust. *Don't touch.*
It keeps better here, in my drawer, than outdoors
Where the air might turn it wrong. Now let's talk
As we hear the rake drag small debris, the crack of twigs;
The ocean water as it drips from empty nets,
The murmur at an accident as the crowd
Turns away from a gone situation; a sound
That's only us, that we put up with, like a crying
In the leaves at night, that rises once, then drops.

Habitual Effacement

The way you tuck yourself in, won't eat.
Toy stars are entirely yours, but your mouth, grim
in a grownup way. Which of us comes second?

Take your crying: I, too, starve with a turned-in face
jammed up against a feast. Pitiful? I'll show you pitiful—
a fractured animal, neutered of trust.

This is only what we are. Let's make disbelief
a fueling, a life-work of bite and swelling.
There are always two in a well-run affliction.

Two, stained private.

In this botched and sunken neighborhood
where the tongue is squandered,
I am barely a mumble, but entirely yours.

I can prove it.

Come out swinging.
Come out burnt and expelled.
Let go with criminal pleasure, all eyed.
Rogue and uninformed,
the curious slide of us is near-perfect.

Then Storm

Clamant with spread noise, the air itself
kept our heads, our bodies toward
its closing scatter until rain
worked over sky. I would not give
in to it the way summer's ground,
its crumbled ochre flushed to mud, would.
Then you said, *I'm sorry*, wanted me
to pardon you, as if I hadn't.

That argument I can't remember
was our last. That the trees were nocent,
exposed to what could crack them wrong
and that our roof, unguttered, let down
a sudden sluice as from a milk cow's split
fullness—I remember that. And how the neighbor's
wire was live and sizzling on the lawn, how
it plumed the night, the blue in it that wasn't fire.

Late Disturbance

Treated with chalk and medical salt,
feigning misgiving, tears—is this complaint

or welcome? I am not easily taught.
What bound us now deforms us.

Here, it's in your chart: your grip replaced
by shriven hands, your sight by one fixed eye.

We've sent such a ruse between us:
small-talked, constricted, endured.

Now in your third step, paltry and shorn,
you stand wondering what's in the ground.

Let steep for years, like chokeback,
under the throat's warm cloth
is a tumult rife with intention, a whole body
disturbed by thought. And your mouth,

well-stained with carmine. As from an astringent
and black-red fruit.

And Everywhere Remembered

Talk to my body after I die.
What's lived is merchandise, spotted
with sun, left under a punctured awning.

Extract a tonic from my slack limbs,
something contagious.
Pampered in death, fanned by a dynasty

of temper, I will burn nicely in your dry house,
the one of dust. In the funeral you hold,
the pall will be an emery cloth, polishing.

Fashion a purity of me, an icon,
amid mantic lamentations.
What the disremembered use not to recede—

smoldering the hills all evening,
crackling sticks, spilling leaves—
I will, also. To be with you.

II

Fundamental Voodoo

In the body's long rembrance,
he stirs: born of fracture and hand-mark,
bled through, part sheet, part stone.

How can he bear the dim and ill, the priest
dissembling to god? The hand-held executions,
the chalice of coughing and gall? In our fever

to bring him back, palms and candles held high
we all look worse—unhealed. A smoke tosses forth
into stained glass light. In the look of a man

unable to speak is something that darkens a room.
Display your dolls, holy and crude, lids fluttering
at the monstrance. Pray him back to his home

of stone where all four windows are scratched
with crosses, where water sprinkled at all four corners
will settle him, struggling, down.

Down House

That Beasley. He got some bug.
Says he can't come out.
See him at the window? He has to watch
while we rake and fetch, repair his fence—
and his daughter, his wife—sure, you heard.
One's lost, he keeps the other locked up.

All the fruit's tucked in that we tended in sun.
Some rotten. He suffers from that. And brother,
he gets the memory of horse, and you catch him
down there, his pants rolled up, on the shore
where they first burst to foam, where their
bodies showed up days later. They're gone.
But he keeps going back.

Why don't he buy more horses, he's got an empty barn.
Why don't he—quick, look busy!
I tell you, this land's blighted with daughter.

Never found but a handful of hair.
She kept a doll of him up in the loft,
out there, with the horses. Why didn't she talk?
Except to the wife. That's what Beasley said,
tormented her bad, wouldn't leave her alone.
So they took her down to the backyard well
put a bag on her head, pushed her down.

Then the horses, gone strange.
What drove *them* to drown?

That child kept her hair down over her face.
Shoulders thrust forward. That's how she walked.
What's marriage without a child? But you know
what they say: a husband comes first.

The Bowl She Drank From

I'll show you the bowl she drank from.
Eyes being covered by bandage.
Fingers unable to spoon.
Being independent of human.

I'll show you the floor she sat on.
Empty of shoe, in the childhood way.
For she was growing small and good.
This being her sunken royalty. This being

her place of true. I'll show you her bracelet of eye
and clasp, put to the wrist without surcease.
Without surcease and foreign. This being a hinge,
constructed to shut, closed at one end

or held open. And this, her mouth and her feeding.
Without preparation, performed by me.
Hidden from sight, oncoming.
And she, with her neck stretched toward.

She, so solemn and halfway dressed.
I'll show you the napkin she gave me,
mistaking it for a dollar.
Not what she wanted to give.
And me, unable to tell her.

The Mummies of Wieuwerd

Since 1609 four corpses and a few birds suspended above
have been lying under a little church in the Netherlands.
The bodies have remained well preserved. Tourists come
to view them regularly.

Gone small in their shut vault, dirt-
lodged in a chancel, they are close
enough to teach the properties of bodies.

No more turbulent circlings or late-
candling autumn leaves disturb them.
Under saints, under footsteps

of the altar-addicted, a choir
mistaking paralysis for holiness,
they are denied decay.

In the face you can see it:
wrinkles heaped like tiny ladders,
a stalled exodus of possession.

Bald and modestly turned, one is so
tubercular you can see through him,
abdomen to back. And strung above,

a row of ornaments upside down:
canaries, starlings, a parrot hung
by one leg frayed as burnt rope.

What wanted to hurt them? This cause
not outside us, its abandoned damage—
merely looking makes us receptacle.

The Candle Effect

In every room you told me *no,*
made talk till your face fell calm and far.

Lie down and cool, you tell me now
as if to predict a blaze.

In anger and brandy I wake
to find myself on fire

except for a slippered foot.

Hot ashes in my robe.
Spotted with burns from beneath.
And how was this done to me—

no one said.

Animal with one call,
they found me in lowered eyelids.
And how would they hoist me from what I made,

that corner of buckling and heat?
The world is a wedding, they said,
an elegant arc describes it. Those tenders,

with flashlights, who took me, blandly adapting
new faces, to a sanctum with no further entry.
Keep secret that house, its consumption.

The Story

Came out wet and lacerated.
Came out unlocated.
Came out close-throated and dusted,
grit filling all the gaps imperfectly filled
with fire, taking our god where he would take
us, abruptly inducted into foreign heaven,
our designated hitler roaring smoke
down the stair, wheelchairs gripped,
unable to manage small tolerances.
Came out heat-smitten,
piecemeal, a throb, a panting
to live, all seeing farther for the first time.
Came out running until we stopped
to look back where metal stood attached
at an angle, where the story would hinge on
air pockets, candles, corpse-sniffing
dogs and those flimsy panels
of our blown-out honeycomb.

Constructing Easter

A number of lunar months, a fatherly
apparatus of nailed-in gold; gall
on a stick, bottled soul. Rosaries greased
with whatever your fingers have rolled.

The armholes pinch and the brace of a hat
is pincered, unkind on the scalp. From this
comes longevity, gratitude. Serious music
and unwanted food. Can someone protect us

from moldering? From the indwelling organs'
revolt? From a sibling's toenails and teeth
encapsuled inside a crust? All the amber fossils are
fallen to private hands. The marrow can't regrow.

Should we join the new-coated coffle
as they shuffle the path to Rome, or go home
and paint another egg. Sip from a caudle.
Warm by a candle. Worship the fertile rabbit, and alone.

III

Insomniac

In a night lit by snow
I saw four black holes
in a fir tree.
One rose up into a crow.
I couldn't sleep
for the other three.

In My Residual Wax and Pitch

Mild month, kind to my face,
make a swaddle of joy and fog
for every nascent bulb. Soften me
through the moistening night

where a small white church
in bas-relief takes another underling,
a listener for what survives decay
and worsening repairs.

Not awe, but the stilled life, the lesson,
the holly sprig, holy and sharp.
I have undergone considerable change
where nothing is fond or tender.

Cut for its scent and standing,
grave as a widow

precise in her bearing,
the tree, in another grief.

I have been away so long,
memory pinches,
its zest relumed. Talk to me now.
Enter this room.

Not Touching Any River

Road of bees I am walking you.
Stinging without a sound.

Of what can be seen in the underbrush,
in its tumble-down crackle of browns

Is a wing, hard away, is a catch of bones.
From wanting after, no relief.

Justice, a feast of air. Make a case
for the human. Try. Live without motion,

a pair of eyes. Careful, I bend
and tap sand from my shoe. Tap sand

from my shoe. Unbend. Only smoke
from a burning shore shows where

the town has been. Not touching any river,
how does the boat travel on.

In the farther room is a listening door.
My bed. The sheet torn down.

Hibernal

One stone crowds another,
Farther on. The silver chair of moon
Tips back and nightlight moves
To tap the ant hole, tend the birch.
We gather to each other and prepare.

Where cash and bottle, salve and sex
Are spent, March will tumble
Us to spring—a crease of tears, a hole
In our new cloth. The meat is gone,
And we are ill.

As moon depends on change,
From bed of veils to forehead fired with gold,
So down the plush of flesh the mending
Worm will stitch—a chronic death,
Bright as orchards staggered on a hill.

Taking the Cure

Dr. Gripsack, a gesture of welcome,
lay your hand here, on my chest.
You say there's a firmament morbid
with angels? I never went there—
yet. Pampered, I guess,
never do what I should.
Want autumn to shed me instead.
In a shimmy of wind-clothes, a tint
of apple, a dementia freely
delivered. I'll be rudimentary as pelt.
Subsisting on berries. A shoate.

Unable to get things done, I might as well
stick out my tongue to the rain.
I might as well pay you in human coin.
Take this garage and its golden junk—
its slits for the rifles' downward fire,

the weapons diagram bitten
by rodents, the hand-knotted helmet
and boots (work of my mother's fingers,
the idolized cloth of her looms)—
go soak them in fire. Dry them in smoke.
Then give me a blanket and carriage,
drawn by two sorrels abreast. A dose
of October's attar, its small, unregarded sun.
I want to be simple again.

Nothing Sweet

What can I have, now that I can't have eggs
or hollow rabbits, eager on hind legs
the popped-out white surprise
of animal candy eyes,
or the jewels of Easter, jelly beans,
strewn amid the shiny green
basket grass—the ache of all that
taste, put out for me. It couldn't last.

A brace of buds and early clusters stand
where foot of root puts firmly into ground
and dizzy bees bump into air—stop and start—
while squirrels compulsive, thread the yard—
for something, they wind up and down the oak,
as stars stay on at morning, and one stroke
of wings brings down the nervous bird
to listen for a squirming in the dirt.

No chocolate, nothing sweet to eat,
I watch the days go off to sleep.

Childhood's diorama:
family plots and shrinking dramas,
tableau doves and fragile lambs;
from behind a rock, the sparkly risen man,
and I see myself through the sugared eye—tiny, aged—
feeling along the candy lawn, blind as an egg.

The Garden of Slow Demise

When the years were tall I walked through them
dumb with delight and blind, past the oak's high
root, and the tree of pleading hands.

Halfway to school was my stopping spot: child-seat
dented in rock. I watched the cat
sway through grass long as a woman's hair.

Into the smell of rubber and wool,
to my wooden desk bolted in place
I opened the top with its shiver

of hinge, to the privacy under its lid.
This was the daily blade of my mind:
the scissors' rasp and squeak

the growl of the sharpener
grinding down to lead.

So soon the unspoken gathers—

a garden of ticks and weeds
and crows, like clerics strolling a parish
declaiming their office aloud. I walk this garden
of seeded spires, hear the wind
unlocking the leaves, and behind it
the chalky tooth biting down,

the shiver of my name—
the way it scraped as I wrote it across the slate.

Diminishing Returns

Don't we talk small when grudge gets
hotly into folds of skin and lodges there.
At the end of my phone cord you loom

so I home in: sense your set of mouth
and back, still at the kitchen window,
your washing silhouette, your careful

staying there. And me upset
beside the cabinets, aware of how the sun
doles panes of winter light, mean

and pale along the greenish walls. Dead
still, as if an ant will find its voice
and tell you how it feels down on the floor.

No mind of mine can matter; no
anger rattles glass, no

one grabs the knife out of its rack. I go

dumb, just breathing into this black
cord, my ear gone numb with listening,
my eye fixed to an opening, an attic, staring dolls.

Let

August brought the slow flies, tropical
thoughts, a stick-figure insect, rigid on the walk.
Then the lilies multiplied.

The way they grew rife, each owning evening
inside, to finally pull off in one shrivel,
soft, between finger and thumb—

their way is mine. I have no wish
to strive. Instead, I take the morning,
make myself a standing place, deliberately

out of the sun. Let sky release its blue crush.
Let rain click its needles of uselessness.
Let lightning sew the piece. Let the rest rinse grass.

When Grass

When grass, like the back of an old dog,
gets matted and whorled, straw-brown,
and from erosion and winter rot
the pond reeds wag their feathered crowns,
it's then we remember who can't come home,
and how long they've been gone.

As we tuck sticks tightly into the fire
and the smolder burns punk and kohl
and we see flung handfuls of birds turn back,
quick, on a shimmered edge, it's then
we worry the dead will come back
to beds untended and wronged.

These fields of loss are stark
with holes too cold for mouse or snake
and we walk on a mix of stalk and weed,
tugging our tumbril of known mistakes.
A bag of fog drags over the grass
its colors of bandage, milk, and remorse.

IV

Wilbur

He took no backtalk
knocked back his scotch
ate pickled pig's feet
fast. His balled socks
flew and he could mock
you into a fine shame.

What shut behind his face,
shut hard. No prying now:
he is stopped. Thought lodged
in him like a snapped branch
stuck in the crook of a good tree
and no divination of stubbed butts

chicken bones, or flecks of soup
can reveal him to us. *Stone
dead.* That E.M.T's rude remark
must be reported, Winifred said,
and the unused hearing aid
(which cost a lot) returned.

Wilbur is Leaving

For all the world a cantankerous
body of pinned-on clothes—I am a stand-in.
For me. And this is what holds me together
and this is what takes me apart:
the shot, the hot rush, the hole
through the heart. I am inconsolable.
All great salesmen are.

In this kind of winter, one step
from the street, bewilderment rules
the house: Ed Sullivan's graveyard face,
dogs on their hind legs, in skirts—
When it's done, I lie down, awake.

The way things happen without me,
and the way things disappear—
you'd think we had thieves, or mice.

Doesn't that frost your ass.
In the morning I see their prints
scrambled across the walk.

Don't try to stop me.
I'm going without you, sheets torn
and wrapped on my feet.
My broken-clock face is unreadable.
My journey is toward what's been lost.
All great journeys are.

Wilbur's Return

Not able to stand, but standing
Back among you
I am as I was, only blanched.

Not of this world,
Wanting to talk, I am
Simply scalded from walking

Fire. The air I carry, blackdamp.
Kindled alone and wrapped
As if in a tight, hot sheet

And my body so cold inside it.
I have missed you.
Or something like you-—

Perhaps the scatter of hay-high grass,
Its frivolous unseeding. Or a flash
Of jack-in-the-pulpit—

The flutter and wobble of that.
Once I tamped down
Denatured earth, all for a root to take hold.

How similar was my life—

The rampant touching of vines,
Unwatered lawn grown over, unmown,

My children, and childhood, gone.
And yes, my distinctive cough.
That room, where I kept myself small.

.

Wilbur's Wake

Stay. Not for the chaste hours
but the buzzed ones: cocktail-
mumbo, star-stuck, danced-out and

crammed ones—I mean, what a kick
he was and didn't we laugh? How
did we—in the doomed tick

and fall, shushed halls, slammed
doors, keep our heads up,
eyes down, mouths shut?

He was skunked with head talk,
taking TV umbrage, aroused
only to berate, and

no mystery, finally.
Just a sprung cuckoo taken out,
disconnected one wire at a time

with no door to stand behind.
His hard tumbles, string of miracles
over, he ate the sandwiches provided,

kept out of our way, and now we see
how wronged he was, straightened
and arranged by stranger hands,

mouth pulled down too far, rigid
in some clothes he never wore, no longer
vivid, and against his own.

Winifred Arriving at Heaven's Lobby

You come to us no more than gland, wanting
the odor of comfort. A frill around your voice.
Some trouble in the throat.
On the crook of our arm, you are safely blind.

Settle here in your own wheelchair. Let us speak
in the language of menials: the helmeted virtues,
poverty bread, discipline without cause.
Disarrangement and one good coat—stand up.

We will help you into it. Because your wardrobe was taken
and driven away in the trunks of cars,
because your golf clubs were set on the walk,
your collected wigs on the lawn,

because your bed is not your own—

let us speak to you of hoarded fire, the body's consolation.
You are backed into night and will go no further
until after a long time. For you who rely on sound

alone, we examine your room
for noises, the close approach of the witless.
Do not prevent us. All we see is damage where
before, there was nothing to break.

Winifred's Blessing

Not all of us become luminous
enough. And for those few, it shows

in the face. As if a burning beneath
the clothing. As if a bride, or a saint.

She is basking in absence, giving
way, who spoke strongly to me

with her hand. Tablet under her tongue,
curled on a cane, she waits

The penny withheld is spent,
I say. Or, rather, I want to say.

Beneficent in her contagion,
holy in all her parts: toenail parings

and talcum, blued filament of a hair.
High and flimsy as iris, nodding

in afternoon, she is the root of me,
deep, and fifty miseries long.

I offer my hand. Almost good enough
for the charred print of her own.

Winifred at St. Anselm's

I'll speak of you first: your rosary lips,
your local destruction and strange energy—
a manifest of backbone and bootstrap, as today

you are interviewed by another beggar
full of medical inquiry. Scorn him. Everything
conspires in this city of pills to make you other

than yourself: a Christian lady, draped in injury
as if dropped into white tallow and burnt
from the wrong end. My unravished bride of moth

and milkpowder, posed against the high window,
still feeding on a diet of tyranny, I see no ecesis,
only dieback and a gaping sleep.

Here are the clothes I brought you.
You know me by my posture.
Now speak of me.

Winifred's Last Look

Sky contracts to one bird
and the cone of evening is lowered,
snuffs day out. You are incapable
of further reduction. Raised, the head

regards you again. Every touch
is a modified blow. Damaged imago,
who could worship, be with her?
Be with her. Be the elder daughter.

Even though, next to such affliction,
your good intention is char. As if to grow,
your gift—cut and no longer fresh—
has been pushed near light

the kind allowed in hospitals
so as not to belittle the sick. Her gaze
is the distance through which you
are dropped. Bad girl to let go.

Winifred is Listening

I am dropping my objects
from a greater height:
Spoon. Needle. Belt.
Blame it on having my fingers pulled straight.
An addiction to hearing things hit.
Blame my eye, where a small eclipse floats.

Another year with a hole at the end—
a tooter, whistling me through
the tribulation of hallways
and other kinds of dark—
my voice in its wafer, its croon,
glued to the top of my tongue.

Meanwhile, up in the lightning, a startle
of silhouettes. The family manikin
jerks and pops, hangs dangling

by the wrists. What head guesses,
body already knows: syringe
and residue, tincture of snow,
an odor of fractible bone.

I've stood near the boxes where
all is made weed. The edge-
sighting, maculate eye
sees what was once sacred, broken,
scarred. These hands. These feet.
This will I go on.

Winifred is Blind

She can't prepare her face.
It shows the tracks and hiding place
of thought. No privacy
behind the stifled smile,
the way she tries to raise herself
from deep within the eye.

Now she can't see me, I see her plain.
Can't break this woman down.
Thatcher-like, her rinsed hair set,
I view her as an undertaker might:
for all the life-like angles, twists of light,
she's through with us, and sprung;

not hobbled by the meals and beds
unmade. She's simple now,
loosened to the sun.

That doughty mouth, a flick of sharp
contempt: I am already gone.
She turns her talk show on.

ESSAYS

I. ON THE PROSING OF POETRY

Why poetry? Or, to put it another way, why not say it in prose? Because the need to say something profound, or new, or significant, or deeply personal, compels us to find a better way of saying it than through prose, our everyday language. Just as the lover turns to uncharacteristic orations and flowery phrases because he senses the inadequacy of everyday speech in the face of new and profound emotion, so our toasts, elegies, special occasion speeches—all of these turn us into poets of the moment as we sense that the vehicle of expression needs to be worthy of its significant subject matter. Nowhere so much as in poetry is the need to communicate something significant, complex or profound coupled so fiercely with the need to communicate it exactly, such that the hearer understands it even to the point of experiencing the original event or emotion him or herself. We turn to poetry—either in poetic forms or in the heightening of prose with poetic devices—when the matter to be expressed threatens to burst the bounds of prose.

This has long been the case. Before writing was invented, poetry was used to mark special occasions and strong emotions and to burn the necessary stories—the myths and truths of a culture—into the memories of the people. Mnemonic devices such as sound, rhythm, and heightened, pictorial language, economy of expression ("epigrammatic" speech that encodes many meanings in as few words as possible) and assonance, consonance, alliteration, parallelism, were the branding irons used for the task. As well, these devices were incantatory, stirring primal responses to their sound and rhythm, and creating an atmosphere for the sacred and magical. Although spoken, poetry was not common; it was instead, a singular kind of speech, reserved for relaying important or sacred events, ensuring that such events would be remembered almost in a physical way, in the body's deep response to sound, rhythm and imagery. Speaking poetically served a purpose. Speaking prosaically also served a purpose—to negotiate everyday reality, to speak of those things which were common to all and not worthy of long remembrance—to speak of the world in transit.

Our ability to write did not erase the distinction. It took contemporary American poets, writing in deliberately flat prose about insignificant personal events and feelings; and editors, publishers and critics dubbing such anecdotes and everyday journal entries "poems," to erase the distinction. We have reached the point we are being asked to believe that a text block, chopped randomly into flat, declarative lines, is a poem. We are told to kneel and stare at this specimen of dead lines laid out in its little coffin on the page, and declare it alive. What do we say?

Although the distinction between prose and poetry as separate genres had already been challenged in Europe by the appearance of the "prose poem"*, in America the distinction was seriously blurred when William Carlos Williams began a new turn in American poetry, a reliance on flat, declarative sentences, the "common speech" of man, and a subsequent eschewing of heightened language and the poetic devices associated with poetry—in short, a turn toward prose—and not even, in many cases, a prose poetic enough to meet the standards of good prose (which includes heightened language and poetic devices to maintain interest):

> **This is Just to Say**
> I have eaten
> the plums
> that were in
> the icebox
>
> and which
> you were probably
> saving
> for breakfast
>
> Forgive me
> they were delicious
> so sweet
> and so cold.

As James Dickey puts it: "How many beginning writers took Williams as their model: were encouraged to write because. Well, if that's poetry, I believe I might be able to write it too!"* And how many people, some forty years later, now look to our Best of American Poetry collections at the millennium's end and, seeing what's there, make the same exclamation?

> She was twenty-five when they settled in our town.
> When they moved from the city into their colonial
> They unpacked wedding china and silver from boxes
> Labeled Tiffany, Bordereau Goodman, and K-Mart.
> Both men and women leaned like peonies
> Toward the luster and power of her unlimited
> Determining smile. They brought with them a small son
> And she bore two daughters in five years.
> She dressed her children in primary colors
> So that they resembled child models in a catalog,
> Yet they played with such charm they made childhood
> Seem happy. Her handsome husband adored her.

> *Smile*, Donald Hall

This "poem" goes on for a total of 106 lines in a block of text separated into paragraphs. In all of these lines, it is only the fifth line ("Both men and women leaned like peonies. etc.") that could reasonably be classified as "poetry" simply because it uses poetic devices—simile (like peonies), internal rhyme (leaned, peonies) consonance (luster, power) and repetition of sounds (unlimited, determining). The rest of the "poem" has been denatured of its poetry. It seems almost deliberate, this boiling off of the images and sounds to leave a monotonous recitation of one bland moment after another. From the same collection:

> The guy picked me up north of Santa Fe
> Where the red hills, dotted with pinon,
> Loop down from the divide into mesas and plain.
> I was standing out there—
> just me, my pack, and the gila monsters—
> when he hauled his Quick off the road
> in a sputter of cinders and dust
> and got out, a gray-bearded, 6-foot, 300-pounder,
> who stretched and said, "Do you want to drive?"

> *Story*, John Balaban

Unlike Hall's poem, which contains one line of poetry, this poem contains zero lines of poetry. Here is what Balaban says about his "poem":

> "A true story. Almost a found poem."

What could this mean? That Balaban titled it "Story" in an ironical, self-conscious way, to make a comment on the state of poetry, much as Warhol's soup cans made a statement on art? That, just as the soup cans were "found" to be art objects, so this anecdote is included in a collection of poetry because it was "found" to be a...what? A poem? But he says it's "almost" a poem. Mysterious as all of this is, the greater mystery is why anyone would choose to think of this anecdote as a poem at all, as implied by its inclusion in The Best American Poetry collection, when it is clearly an anecdote truncated into lines.

Another best poem of 1999 is an anecdote from the poet's teaching experience:

> Once when I was teaching "Dover Beach"
> To a class of freshmen, a young woman
> Raised her hand and said, "I'm confused
> About this 'Sea of Faith.'" "Well," I said,
> "let's talk about it. We probably need
> to talk a bit about figurative language.
> What confuses you about it?"
> "I mean, is it a real sea?" she asked.
> "You mean, is it a real body of water
> that you could point to on a map
> or visit on a vacation?"
> "Yes," she said. "Is it a real sea?"
> Oh Christ, I thought, is this where we are?
> Next year I'll be teaching them the alphabet
> And how to sound words out.

Sea of Faith, John Brehm

This goes on in the same vein for another page. As with Balaban's Story, you read through this tedious personal anecdote unable to believe it is as devoid of meaning, humor or point as it appears, and with nothing in the language, line after line, to redeem it. Its conclusion is sophomoric:

> ...I wished it was true, wished there really was a Sea of Faith
> that you could wade out into,
> dive under its blue and magic waters,
> hold your breath, swim like a fish
> down to the bottom, and then emerge again
> able to believe in everything, faithful
> and unafraid to ask even the simplest of questions,
> happy to have them simply answered.

"Swim like a fish"? Yes, the only poetic device. Enough to make you want to drink like a fish. A simple question I have is: why is this called a poem? Another is: why is it included in a collection of best poems?

Perhaps the most extreme case of stripping the poem of all its identifying characteristics is Robert Creeley's anorexic anecdote *Mitch*:

> Mitch was a classmate
> later married extraordinary poet
> and so our families were friends
> when we were young
> and lived in New York, New Hampshire, France.

In a kind of shorthand, Creeley shoots off one thought fragment after another, blurting them out breathlessly as if to a jogging mate. As William Logan points out:

> "In Creeley we never get a memorable image, a thing seen precisely, a sentence carried as far as thinking will take it. He has eliminated most of the texture of verse, of the pleasurable massing of words. He has at times lost his very taste for sentences and dissolved into the tedium of diary jotting or the Dictaphone."

Thus, by a grand renaming of things—dubbing these pieces "poems"—The *Best American Poetry of 1999* has seemingly set out to single-handedly eradicate what's left of the distinction between prose and poetry. And although a large portion of this collection is composed of anecdotal prose pieces truncated into lines from poets like Jacobik, Kizer, Koertge, Levine, Rich, Thiel, and the poets cited here, it is in Robert Bly's introduction to this collection that we find something even more disheartening: he warns us against the computer, its "cool and empty language" and claims that it's "as if some world wide force were trying to free us all from literary style, and is succeeding."* If so, then the proof of the "force's" success is in the pages of his collection, not on someone's computer screen. As Bly also says in the introduction:

> "Many contemporary writers persuade themselves it is good not to have inwardness, not to have intensity, not to engage layers of meaning not to have pungent phrasings.."

But have the writers persuaded us, the readers? Are we persuaded that these are poems with inwardness, intensity, layers of meaning and so on? Are we persuaded that these are the best by a poet/editor paranoid enough to believe that there is a worldwide force emanating from the computer that will destroy literary style?

How we got here—to a lack of distinction between poetry and prose—by way of William Carlos Williams, and continuing on through hundreds and hundreds of imitators and hundreds and hundreds of imitators of imitators, all long ignorant of their origin is not now so important, as the question: how do we start making the distinction again between poetry and prose? Poets continue to write chopped-up prose and call it poetry, making it the model for newer poets, who then continue the cycle. And, the more we accept that established poets will throw down their journal entries and jottings, their to-do lists and mind doodles, and that editors will publish these, dubbing them, not only poems, but accomplished and brilliant poems, the less able, we, as readers, are to protest. Because we are being told this is a poem by those who "know"—the poet, the editor, the critic and the teacher.

To rebel against the denaturing of poetry into prose, and not just into prose, but in many cases, into badly written and uninteresting prose, seems futile when such renowned poets as Simic can write:

> I never gave them a thought. Years had gone by,
> Many years. I had plenty of other things
> To mull over. This morning I was in the dentist's chair
> When his new assistant walked in
> Pretending not to recognize me in the slightest
> As I opened my mouth obediently...

From *Prison Guards Silhouetted Against the Sky*, Charles Simic

The poet tells himself it's a poem. He tells his editor it's a poem (or perhaps the reverse). His editor tells the publisher it's a poem. Then, they all tell us it's a poem—never has the story of the emperor's new clothes been so meaningful as in American poetry today. Perhaps the most depressing manifestation of the look-ma-no-poetry-in-my-poem! phenomenon is in the actual deterioration of prose itself into the badly written, boring and humorless anecdote:

> A man walks into a bar. You think that's some kind of joke?
> Actually he runs in, to get out of the freezing weather.
> Who cares, you say. Nobody you know.
> You've got your own troubles, could use a drink yourself.
> You get your coat, a long scarf. You trudge
> to the corner over the scraped sidewalk, slip and fall down hard
> on the ice. Actually a banana peel, but who's looking?
> Only a priest, a rabbi, and a lawyer you vaguely recognize—
> didn't she help with the divorce? Never mind, the marriage
> is over, good riddance. You're thinking now
> you'd better have a double...

From *HA*, Kim Addonizio

To reclaim poetry: Where to begin? When to begin? We begin by defining the poem, and we begin now, by defining its effect on us, by its manifestation in us, the trusting and ready to appreciate reader—not in a theory of what poetry should be. We must become poetry empiricists— trusting the knowledge of our own senses and good sense. By its effect we shall know it. For example, in *The Best American Poetry of 1999* is a poem by Dorriane Laux that is not in any traditional poetic form, is written in prose-like sentences, and tells a story—yet it is a poem, and, along with those by Yusef Kimunyakaa and Richard Wilbur, among the best in the collection:

The Shipfitter's Wife

> I loved him most
> when he came home from work,
> his fingers still curled from fitting pipe,
> his denim shirt ringed with sweat
> and smelling of salt, the drying weeds

of the ocean. I'd go to where he sat
on the edge of the bed, his forehead
anointed with grease, his cracked hands
jammed between his thighs, and unlace
the steel-toed boots, stroke his ankles
and calves, the pads and bones of his feet.
Then I'd open his clothes and take
the whole day inside me—the ship's
gray sides, the miles of copper pipe,
the voice of the foreman clanging
off the hull's silver ribs. Spark of lead
kissing metal. The clamp, the winch,
the white fire of the torch, the whistle,
and the long drive home.

Dorriane Laux

A simple story that the poet leads us into, layer by layer, with a master-
ful accretion of detail built around objective imagery, tension in sen-
tence structure and the final astonishing and satisfying conjunction of
opposites—outer and inner, work and rest, conflict and peace, man and
woman, the demands of the world and the demands of love—in a
description of how the outer world, the man himself, is taken in,
absorbed tenderly by the woman, and all of this is made deftly and bril-
liantly into a metaphor for the coming together of this couple in love-
making. There is much internal rhyme and imagery as well as layers of
meaning and significance, while each line earns its place in the overall
structure. The techniques in this poem are invisible. It delivers its effect
before we know what hit us.

There's no doubt that it is important and necessary to declare the
nakedness of the contemporary American poem, to reject the notion that
a poet, renowned or not, can perpetrate this continuing fraud of passing
off their amateurish or unfinished prose jottings as poems. The machin-
ery of publication must have vigilant and knowledgeable editors,
unafraid to publish excellent, unknown poets or to reject inferior poems
from established poets—even their friends. Before they can presume to

make another year-end collection of the best contemporary American poems, they should be sure they have poems to collect.

The following works are cited in this article:

Babel to Byzantium: Poets and Poetry Now, James Dickey
The Best American Poetry of 1999, Guest Editor, Robert Bly
The Prose Poem and the Ideology of Genre, Michel Delville
Charles Simic, Kim Addonizio excerpts from
Poetry International
Reputations of The Tongue, William Logan

II. I=N=C=O=H=E=R=E=N=T: ON LANGUAGE POETRY

When poets shake words and roll them onto the page, they are look-ing for fresh combinations, hoping to evoke new ideas. Meaning—though not necessarily unwelcome—is beside the point. If it appears at all, it is either by accident, or as a result of a reader's Rorschach-like projection. It is not something intended, or "put there," by the poet. For most poets, this is a starting place for a poem. For Language Poets, this is its end.

The need for coherence appears to be basic, perhaps even neurologi-cal. Science has proved the human brain strives to find a pattern, an order, a meaning in chaos. What isn't coherent, we strive to make so. It satisfies us. Thus, before settling for separate, unconnected pieces, beautiful as they may be, we will look hard for connections.

While shapes and colors can become untethered from their represen-tation, or meaning, a poem can only become fully untethered from meaning if it is without words. This is because the smallest irreducible piece—the word—retains meaning, in and out of context. A totally meaningless poem would logically consist of a blank page. In spite of this difficulty, some poets do manage to make extremely close approaches to the state of meaninglessness while still using words:

> & I the magic in her stew
> the north whine abundantly
> saccharine to the chew
> old stairs like all the majesty
> was theirs
> to take a lark
> or flare largely malingering
> adipose aversions
> went right out the finnetre
> into the bowl
> where deceit is not known

& the dumb dance in delight
in the roar of the

"If .Gif Were a Place," Charles Bernstein

This poem is not meaningless in an accidental sense; that is, in the sense that the poet intended to write something coherent but failed. Instead, this poet intends to put words together in a way that defies coherence, because he is a Language Poet. Language Poetry is wordplay, without the play. When poets engage in pure wordplay, they leave meaning to chance or projection; Language Poets, on the other hand, are obsessed with meaning in the same way an atheist is obsessed with God. Every poem is designed to disprove its existence. Why would a poet strive to create incoherence?

According to Bernstein, one of Language Poetry's founders and leading practitioners, such striving produces poetry that is "decentered, community-controlled, taken out of the service of the capitalistic project."[1]

Thus, every poem is another manifestation of certain ideals:

Language poets tend to see language as constructed by relations of power, and not as either transcendent, universal, or natural. Language poets are for the most part intensely interested in literary theory, and thus see the theoretical issues raised by their poetry as a central part of the poetry itself, in contrast to more traditional literary practitioners who think of criticism and theory as descriptive, secondary, and in many cases irrelevant.

In particular, many language poets have noted the way in which grammar structures tend to support the power structures of western societies.

Language poets have also pointed out how traditional European poetic genres and forms tend to naively reflect western values. These writers consciously identify poetry as conditioned by the ideological limitations and power of the written word in western culture. [2]

The Language Poet must construct, not just a poem, but an uberpoem, a poem that does more than "mean" something, a poem that

84

eclipses westernized thought structures, transcends cultural products, and frees minds enslaved by capitalism. Radically PC (Poetically Correct), Language Poets strive to create a new world order, hoping to achieve their goal with such lines as:

> fro appears before us
> The matter is so
> Can we share its kind of existence
> The brink that's the sympathy
> Sound circling point of hearing
> Think how different it is when we come to point of view
> "I" moving about unrolled barking at blue clouds
> devoted to each other?
> To hasten to the point? to evade anxiety? to picture?

From "The manner in which we are present at this time to and" by Lynn Hejinian

Paradoxically, the more incoherent the poem, the more meaningful it is, because it is testament to the fact that "producing" is not the goal—that's a goal fit for a capitalist society, not a Language Poet.

The poem's very incoherence is a protest that "meaning" is a socially constructed, contextual, and therefore, tainted, entity. To capture pre-meaning, or "surface"— the babbling that cannot speak its name—is a nobler goal. In order to save us from the Western capitalist construction called a poem, the Language Poets had to destroy it. But two other possible reasons for writing Language Poetry come to mind:

1. The poet cannot successfully create a coherent poem and so makes a virtue of his failure.

2. The poet cannot successfully create a coherent poem and so uses poem-as-pretext for expounding critical theories—something he or she can do, and that, happy coincidence, ensures an academic career.

To be a Language Poet at the movement's birth in the early '70s, was to be a raiser of consciousness, a radical. And it was so easy to join—no writing required, simply reading one Language Poem was sufficient because doing so "draws the reader into the production process by leaving the connections between various elements open, thus allowing the reader to produce the connections between those elements. In this way, presumably, the reader recognizes his or her part in the social process of production."[3]

The circle is complete. Simply by "reading" a language poem, one became part of the larger political protest. So much less taxing than travelling to Washington to tie oneself to a gate. And, since Language Poetry was democratic, anyone who"believed" in the aims of Language Poetry was also automatically qualified to write it since no voice, awareness of audience, or purpose was required; no cultural constructs such as poetic conventions were used, no poetic traditions were honored, no poetic talent (another worthless cultural construct) was necessary. No meaningful work could therefore be produced. Furthermore, the work could not be measured, judged, rated, ranked or in any way acted upon as a "product." It meant nothing. Staring up at us blankly, thrashing and burbling senselessly, it just was. Pure non-sense.

Armed with an inexhaustible talent for rationalizing their poetic incoherence, Language Poets formed along the roots of traditional poetry like fungi, sprouting a twisted tendril called "The New Sentence." Of course, this new sentence was not really a sentence at all (further evidence of how meanings aren't necessary to the words they come with). As its inventor, Ron Silliman, assured us, "...Each New Sentence gains its disorienting effects by being placed next to another, to which it has, apparently, only tangential relevance." [4]

Thus, the following Language Poem:

> Optimize, categorize, resort to promptness. Every day exacts the cost of drawstring. Evanescence is the goal of gradual removal from a foreground meant to be productive. I chose the color blue to tantalize a setting echoing my bounty. Each workaround leaves evidence of a moments breath.
> A kind of precipice that will mince trickles of completion. Name an animal that does not need to pilfer and resume what you were doing on the high wire. Braying wish worlds cauterize the lively texture of self

worth. I thought the sole prerequisite for rodeo was to be of certain mind. Ink disturbs worlds in the way a polished cleaver frames catastrophe as sequential acts of will

"Desk" by Sheila Murphy

Must be superior to the following non-Language Poem:

> I have known the inexorable sadness of pencils,
> Neat in their boxes, dolor of pad and paper-weight,
> All the misery of manila folders and mucilage,
> Desolation in immaculate public places,
> Lonely reception room, lavatory, switchboard,
> the unalterable pathos of basin and pitcher,
> Ritual of multigraph, paper-clip, comma,
> Endless duplication of lives and objects.
> And I have seen dust from the walls of institutions,
> Finer than flour, alive, more dangerous than silica,
> Sift, almost invisible, through long afternoons of tedium,
> Dropping a fine film on nails and delicate eyebrows,
> Glazing the pale hair, the duplicate grey standard faces.

"Dolor" by Theodore Roethke

Why? Because the first poem produces the desired "disorienting effects." It exists outside of the context of external, socially-imposed, capitalistically-mandated, activity. But the second poem has, in fact, produced something (meaning) and, beautifully constructed though it may be, it is by a language poetry definition, inferior. It has used up its potential in the service of production, served its capitalistic ends and is now tossed like an empty take-out carton in the street—consumed, corrupt and kaput. Leaking with meaning, such writing was actually victimizing us, the readers, holding us hostage to corrupt Western ideals. By contrast, Language Poetry was "....constructive in its demolition of the conventional relationship between the active (dictatorial) writer and the passive (victimized) reader." [5]

The Language Poets restored us to our natural, infantile state of total confusion and, heady with lack of closure, we were sent on our way while they worked to accomplish grander things, to:[6]

1. Systematically derange the language, for example, write a work consisting only of prepositional phrases, or, add a gerundive to every line of an already existing piece of prose or poetry, etc.

2. Get a group of words (make a list or select at random); then form these words (only) into a piece of writing—whatever the words allow.
3. Attempt to eliminate all connotation from a piece of writing & vice versa.

4. Take a traditional text like the pledge of allegiance to the flag. For every noun, replace it with one that is seventh or ninth down from the original one in the dictionary. For instance, the word "honesty" would be replaced by "honey dew melon."

5. Take a piece of prose writing and turn it into poetic lines. Then, without remembering that you were planning to do this, make a poem of the first and last words of each line to see what happens.
For instance, the following lines (from Einstein):

> When at the reception
> Of sense-impressions, memory pictures
> Emerge this is not yet thinking
> And when...

Would become:

> When reception
> Of pictures
> Emerge thinking
> And when...

6. Attempt writing in a state of mind that seems least congenial.
Like the Dadaists before them, but lacking their flair, fun, creativity, and talent, Language Poets used their work as a statement about the culture in which it was created. They made readers hip to the act of the poet, the use of the word, and the dependence on context for meaning. Unfortunately, they didn't stop there. They continue even now to

> "...reject coherence based on the human standard since that [coherence] has already been determined, given a position in the hierarchy of capi-

talist society." [7]

We miss the coherence that meets human needs. Meanwhile, the point of incoherence becomes clearer: to secure an academic career position in the hierarchy of capitalist society.

NOTES:

1. "Textual Politics and the Language Poets", George Hartley
2. "Language and Postlanguage Poetries", Mark Wallace
3. "Textual Politics and the Language Poets", George Hartley
4. "Poetry of Play, Poetry of Purpose: The Continuity of American Language Poetry", John R. Woznicki
5. "Textual Politics and the Language Poets", George Hartley
6. "Advice given to budding L=A=N=G=U=A=G=E P=O=E=T=S", Bernadette Mayer
7. "Poetics, Polemic, and the Question of Intelligibility", Benjamin Friedlander

III. The Argument for Silence

Like a religious order, but without the religion, poets are fueled by deep connections to the ineffable, an inner silence. Their tendency toward introspection and close observation, coupled with an almost physiological need for reverie is, by necessity, held in suspension by the tasks and concerns of daily life. Retreats like Yaddo and MacDowell exist as evidence of the need for a place for poets to go and replenish, but such places also implicitly expect them to produce something. The only real retreat for some unfortunate poets has been in a hospital, where nothing at all is expected except getting well. Can't poets take a break?

The tension between 'career' and 'vocation' in poetry is nowhere more obvious than in academia where poets take a sabbatical in order to write poetry, but never take a sabbatical from writing poetry. I believe that a certain variety of established poet, perhaps those with a substantial number of books, would benefit greatly from a poetry sabbatical. There is evidence of a need for poetic silence all around us. We see it every time we read a denatured poem by a renowned poet, usually in a renowned publication; evidence that the enabling editors of such publications have failed in their duty to enforce last call.

For example, poets James Tate, Philip Levine and Mary Oliver have each produced more than 16 books of poetry. Whatever has driven this production, it is clear from the trajectory of all three poets that something must stop it. In all three cases, a windiness, a wordiness, a kind of poetic logorrhea can be found in their latest work in contrast to the fire and compression in their early work. Flatlined, barely pulsing, their latest work is being kept alive by extraordinary means: the artificial resuscitation of continuous publication.

Are poets afflicted with the same burn-out syndrome as their corporate counterparts? The same laziness as their successful bourgeois pals? Can they reach their poetic Peter Principle? I say yes. Take Tate. His early work was nothing if not passionate and inventive. His voice was both fantastical and lyrical, putting us deftly into a dream of life that was realer than life in its portents, regrets and tragic humor. For example, this excerpt is from the title poem of his first book:

The Lost Pilot
for my father, 1922-1944

> Your face did not rot
> like the others—the co-pilot,
> for example, I saw him
>
> yesterday. His face is corn-
> mush: his wife and daughter,
> the poor ignorant people, stare
>
> as if he will compose soon.
> He was more wronged than Job.
> But your face did not rot
>
> like the others--it grew dark,
> and hard like ebony;
> the features progressed in their
>
> distinction. If I could cajole
> you to come back for an evening,
> down from your compulsive
>
> orbiting, I would touch you,
> read your face as Dallas,
> your hoodlum gunner, now,
> with the blistered eyes, reads
> his braille editions. I would
> touch your face as a disinterested
>
> scholar touches an original page.

The amazing image of the dead father, orbiting like a cast-off god, the surrealism of the son's imaginings and his enormous yearning for the father, the control of emotion and deft line breaks—all of these qualities stand in contrast to Tate's offering from the latest issue (#53) of Agni:

The Florist

I realized Mother's Day was just two days
Away, so I went into the florist and said, "I'd
Like to send my mother a dozen long-stem red
Roses." The guy looked at me and said, "My mother's
Dead." I thought this was highly unprofessional
Of him, so I said, "How much would that be?" He
Wiped his eyes and said, "Oh, that's all right. I'm
Over it, really. She never loved me anyway, so why
Should I grieve." "Can they be delivered by Thursday?"
I inquired. "She hated flowers," he said. "I've
Never known a woman to hate flowers the way she did.
She wanted me to be a dentist, like her father.
Can you imagine that, torturing people all day.
Instead, I give them pleasure. She disowned me,
Really. And yet I miss her," and then he started
Crying again. I gave him my handkerchief and he
Blew his nose heartily into it. My annoyance had
Given way to genuine pity. This guy was a mess.
I didn't know what to do. Finally I said, "Listen,
Why don't you send a dozen roses to my mother. You
Can tell her you are a friend of mine. My mother
Loves flowers, and she'll love you for sending them
To her." He stopped crying and scowled at me. "Is
This some kind of trick? A trap or something, to
Get me tied up in a whole other mother thing, because
If it is, I mean, I just got rid of one, and I can't
Take it, another I mean, I'm not as strong as I
Appear…" "Forget it," I said, "it was a bad idea,
And I'm certainly not sending my mother any flowers
This year, that too was a bad idea. Will you be
all right if I leave now, I have other errands, but
if you need me I can stay." "Yes, if you could stay
with me a while. My name is Skeeter and Mother's
Day is always such a trial for me. I miss her more
Every passing day," he said. And so we sat there
Holding hands for an hour or so, and then I was on
My way to the cleaners, the bank and the gas station.

This piece is representative of work showing up nowadays by Tate: anecdotal, prosy, and obviously tossed-off. The wry humor is a small echo from his past work and does little to compensate for the loss of passion, surrealistic flights of fancy, dark and powerful humor and language compression of his first books.

Yet, Tate continues to produce and editors continue to publish what he sends as if nothing's wrong. But something is wrong. There is a marked deterioration in quality. When it began or why it began is not as important as why it continues to be published. Are editors simply skipping the part where they evaluate the poem? Since editors enable Tate's current output by continuing to publish anything he writes no matter what the quality, he needs to stop sending his work out. He has now published enough books and enough poems in journals and magazines to satisfy his readership and to ensure a legacy, a place in the "canon." Now he needs to be quiet before he becomes the dinner guest who has too much to drink and won't stop talking. Our attention has waned, because his attention has waned. Soon, we will all need to go home. I suggest he precede us.

Philip Levine began his poetic career with poems of such passion, social consciousness and tender lyrical portaiture that it is painful to read his tepid imitations of himself. With the brilliance of "Animals are Passing From Our lives" and "They Feed they Lion" still present in our consciousness of contemporary poetry, it creates a cognitive dissonance in us to read his latest work, like this one, excerpted from his most recent collection, *The Mercy*:

The Return

All afternoon my father drove the country roads
between Detroit and Lansing. What he was looking for
I never learned, no doubt because he never knew himself,
though he would grab any unfamiliar side road
and follow where it led past fields of tall sweet corn
in August or in winter those of frozen sheaves.
Often he'd leave the Terraplane beside the highway
to enter the stunned silence of mid-September,

his eyes cast down for a sign, the only music
his own breath or the wind tracking slowly through
the stalks or riding above the barren ground. Later
he'd come home, his dress shoes coated with dust or mud,
his long black overcoat stained or tattered
at the hem, sit wordless in his favorite chair,
his necktie loosened, and stare at nothing. At first
my brothers and I tried conversation, questions
only he could answer: Why had he gone to war?
Where did he learn Arabic? Where was his father?
I remember none of this. I read it all later,
years later as an old man, a grandfather myself,
in a journal he left my mother with little drawings
of ruined barns and telephone poles, receding
toward a future he never lived, aphorisms
from Montaigne, Juvenal, Voltaire, and perhaps a few
of his own: "He who looks for answers finds questions."
....

Levine needs to put the paragraphs back into his writing and market this
kind of piece as a memoir. His output now consists of stories and
remembrances, and, while lovely, touching, even poetic, these pieces are
being misrepresented as poems.

Levine has reached his peak, has received the Pulitzer Prize, the
National Book Award, the American Book Award, and the National
Book Critics Circle Award. He has mastered the combination of social
consciousness and poetic sensibility, given us jolts of beauty mixed with
outrage and compassion. Many of his poems will surely be remembered
and studied by future generations. He can take a break now. But who
will let him know it's OK to find his silence, to replenish his poetic
voice, to change, or even to stop—if not writing, then at least publish-
ing? Probably no one.

The case of Mary Oliver is a bit different in that her poetry hasn't
changed much in its quality; it began and continues in the same
medium-register with the same nature themes and techniques, the same
"inspirational" philosophy. The poems are competent, well-made and
full of "beautiful thoughts." Unfortunately, as in the previous examples,
she shows no sign of letting up after more 16 volumes of poetry, the

Pulitzer Prize, the National Book Award, the Lannan Literary Award, and the New England Book Award for Literary Excellence. In her earlier work there is some attempt at compression and close poetic observation as in this very popular, much published poem from Dream Work, published in 1986:

Wild Geese

You do not have to be good.
You do not have to walk on your knees
for a hundred miles through the desert repenting.
You only have to let the soft animal of your body
love what it loves.
Tell me about despair, yours, and I will tell you mine.
Meanwhile the world goes on.
Meanwhile the sun and the clear pebbles of the rain
are moving across the landscapes,
over the prairies and the deep trees,
the mountains and the rivers.
Meanwhile the wild geese, high in the clean blue air,
are heading home again.
Whoever you are, no matter how lonely,
the world offers itself to your imagination,
calls to you like the wild geese, harsh and exciting—
over and over announcing your place
in the family of things.

Here are the elements that will re-appear, over and over again in Oliver's work, the bird(s) or beast(s) that represent the poet's spirit/self; the plain-spoken images, the conversational, intimate tone, the good-to-the-last-drop spoonful of life's medicine, cherry-flavored so it goes down easy. I predict that this particular poem will become our next "Desiderata" a framed version of which will be read and pondered from many a middle-class toilet seat. The main virtue of "Wild Geese" and of Oliver's earlier work is its brevity. In her later work, while never departing from her new-age bromides, Oliver finds it necessary to say the same things with even more words, as if her stature demands a higher and higher word count. Here, a few excerpts from the interminable poem Flare, illustrates the point:

Flare

1.

Welcome to the silly, comforting poem.
It is not the sunrise,
which is a red rinse,
which is flaring all over the eastern sky;
it is not the rain falling out of the purse of God;
it is not the blue helmet of the sky afterward,
or the trees, or the beetle burrowing into the earth;
it is not the mockingbird who, in his own cadence,
will go on sizzling and clapping
from the branches of the catalpa that are thick with blossoms,
   ·   that are billowing and shining,
that are shaking in the wind.

2.

You still recall, sometimes, the old barn on your great-grandfather's farm, a place you
    visited once,
and went into, all alone, while the grown-ups sat and talked in the house.
It was empty, or almost. Wisps of hay covered the floor, and some wasps sang at the windows, and maybe there was
a strange fluttering bird high above, disturbed, hoo-ing a little and staring down from a messy ledge with wild,
binocular eyes.
Mostly, though, it smelled of milk, and the patience of animals; the give-offs of the body were still in the air, a vague
ammonia, not unpleasant.
Mostly, though, it was restful and secret, the roof high up and arched, the boards unpainted and plain.
You could have stayed there forever, a small child in a corner, on the last raft of hay, dazzled by so much space that
seemed empty, but wasn't
Then—you still remember—you felt the rap of hunger—it was noon—and you turned from that twilight dream and
hurried back to the house, where the table was set, where an uncle patted you on the shoulder for welcome, and
there was your place at the table.

3.
Nothing lasts.
There is a graveyard where everything I am talking about is,
now.
I stood there once, on the green grass, scattering flowers.

I bury her
in a box
in the earth
and turn away.
My father
was a demon of frustrated dreams,
was a breaker of trust,
was a poor, thin boy with bad luck.
He followed God, there being no one else
he could talk to;
he swaggered before God, there being no one else
who would listen.
Listen,
this was his life.
I bury it in the earth.
I sweep the closets.
I leave the house.
....

12.
When loneliness comes stalking, go into the fields, consider
the orderliness of the world. Notice
something you have never noticed before,
like the tambourine sound of the snow-cricket
whose pale green body is no longer than your thumb.

Stare hard at the hummingbird, in the summer rain,
shaking the water-sparks from its wings.

Let grief be your sister, she will whether or no.
Rise up from the stump of sorrow, and be green also,
like the diligent leaves.

A lifetime isn't long enough for the beauty of this world
and the responsibilities of your life.

Scatter your flowers over the graves, and walk away.
Be good-natured and untidy in your exuberance.
In the glare of your mind, be modest.
And beholden to what is tactile, and thrilling.

Live with the beetle, and the wind.

This is the dark bread of the poem.
This is the dark and nourishing bread of the poem.

In this one we find a lobotomized Theodre Roethke, William Stafford afflicted with a bad case of speechifying, and Kahil Gibran weeping by a toadstool. Welcome to the silly, comforting poem.

With the market for poetry so narrow, the poetry prizes so sparse, the audience for poetry so small, and the number of new and talented poets so large, I wonder why quality of work is not more of a criterion for publication.

Why do poets who have published 16 books and counting, who have won major prizes and firmly established their reputations, continue to be published as their work deteriorates? Are we witnessing the poetic equivalent to *Whatever Happened to Baby Jane* with our celebrity poets shuffling through their lines, turning their early achievement into a parody of itself? The celebrity actors do it for money. But what keeps the celebrity poet publishing? We can guess what keeps the editors publishing them: name-brand recognition. We can guess what keeps the public buying their books: name-brand recognition. We can guess to whom emerging poets look when learning their craft: name-brand models. And so we have a cycle that is ultimately destructive to poetry itself: Escher-like, the copiers copy the copiers, each generation producing worse poetry until the poetic landscape is filled with a lurching multitude of poet-steins. Soon angry readers will be pursuing with torches and pitchforks.

These well-established poets are long overdue to either take a break from writing, or to write purely for their own satisfaction—if they can remember when that was enough—and to stop crowding an already over-crowded poetry marketplace. They can also take on more of a role nurturing young talent. The gatekeepers and tastemakers have failed to stop the cycle of devolution. It's up to the poets themselves.

IV. The Best I Can Do This Year: Lehman's Best American Poetry, 2001

Here it is again: that annual Rubik's cube of a collection we rush to buy, eager to hold each poem to the light, only to aimlessly flip pages this way and that, finally closing the book in resigned bafflement, placing it next to the other unsolved collections in this series. Next year, will we rush to buy it again?

It's a yearly tradition, this snuffed prelude to Christmas where every poem is opened in hope and discarded in despair. No book of poetry raises so much expectation—and lets us down so hard. The Best American Poetry is the Best American Paradox we have; from its title, to its foreword, to the content itself.

Consider how the title promises a winnowing out, a narrowing down, the most worthwhile use of our precious time; a competition, a rating, exemplary models—in short, winners. Once past the gilt-edged sign, however, we are in a suburban poetry mall, wandering and foot-tired, eyes caught by bits of glitter here and there, everything turning into nothing-I-want or unable-to-find. Then the inevitable questions: why did these poems win? What rating system was used? How were the sources for them selected? Does anybody like these poems?

We understand "best" in relation to the Olympics—but what does the word "best" mean here? We don't know. And worse, we shouldn't have asked. As we enter the poetry manager's office of the Foreword, David Lehman—series editor and motivational speaker—wants us to see that there is no real best—or, if there is, we shouldn't desire it. What we should desire instead is the proliferation of poetry throughout the land, an increase of poets, an increase of readers, an increase of writing programs. Poetry, Lehman assures us, is on the rise in America. In the same way that each generation is taller, reaches puberty sooner, lives longer, and is more affluent than the previous ones, so does the impulse to write and publish poetry grow stronger, the need to attend creative writing workshops become more pressing. Poetry is every American's birthright and the mission of poetry managers, like Lehman, is clear: "to nurture talent and keep the love of poetry at its liveliest, most receptive, and most creative state, and if the student publishes few poems but becomes an avid reader we will have done a job that others have relinquished."

That is to say, the job of convincing people they are poets, and to pay for the privilege of being so convinced. If they publish few poems, that's fine, as long as they buy books of poems and keep the poet managers alive.

To be the best means that there are others less than best, a conclusion Lehman must obscure in his Foreword. Such a conclusion might demoralize the poet work force. Therefore, he champions the practice of poetry in all corners of American society, gathers data on the occurrence of poetry lines quoted by basketball players, media stars and other public figures—proving that even famous people have fragments of poems embedded in them like shrapnel from their school days.

It is not clear what his roster of famous-people-who-know-a-line-of-poetry-and-maybe-even-write-some proves, other than that they are like everyone else. Maybe that's the point—we shouldn't feel bad if we're not "high culture" 'cause even our celebrities are cool with not having any real knowledge or understanding of poetry. Doesn't stop them from being poets. Lehman reminds us that we are a nation of poets, and that everyone is born with the inalienable right to attend a creative writing program.

Before handing to Robert Hass—guest editor for this volume—the job of reconciling the title of this series with the philosophy in its Foreword, Lehman poses the overarching paradox of the project: "The Best American Poetry is committed to the notion that excellence in poetry is not incompatible with the pursuit of a general audience." Paradoxical, because, committed or not, this series has achieved the distinction of making excellence in poetry irrelevant, and thereby, the pursuit of a general audience impossible. What general audience, for example, would admire these lines?

102

I thought I saw a turtledove resting in a waffle.
Then I saw it was a rat doing something awful.[1]

Who would deem them "excellent"? There is no incompatibility—any general audience would perceive, correctly, that the lines are drivel. End of pursuit.

Pity Robert Hass then, as he awakens one bright summer morning, full of purpose, as, cup of coffee in hand, he begins to "...take out the boxes of marked-up magazines and xeroxes of poems from magazines, my own markings and the xeoroxes and notations of the indefatigable David Lehman, and try to find what I was looking for."

As Hass shuffles through his boxes, day after day, worrying that he has no "principle of selection" and that in the absence of one, he needs to make his own taste "definitively is thrown into a state of doubt:

"Some days I liked nothing. I had no clear sense how much of this was mood, and how much the quality of the work I happened to be reading."

Perhaps Hass's mood played a part in the selection of "Doubt" by Fanny Howe, a three-and-a-half-pager filled with lines of such memorable music as:

Virginia Woolf committed suicide in 1941 when the German bombing campaign against England was at its peak and when she was reading Freud whom she had staved off until then.

Anyone who tries, as she did, out of a systematic training in secularism, to forge a rhetoric of belief is fighting against the odds. Disappointments are everywhere waiting to catch you, and an ironic realism is always convincing.

Hope seems to resist extermination as much as a roach does.[2]

(plus three more reader-numbing pages)

As the project progressed, perhaps a darker mood descended, as reflected in Alice Notley's four-and-a-half page, unpunctuated run-on sentence of a poem which needs to be read holding the book sideways:

> if its a spiritual offense does it as wrongdoing take place more in more
> in the
> second
>
>   leftover
>   or spiritual world and is the significance of the double now that i
> might be
>   might the
>   one who offends in other circumstance or that it takes two to make an
> offense
>   but how
>   was i used and why were the others not usable was it because they
> were always too [3]

(plus four and a half more small type, sideways, reader-numbing pages)

Finally, Hass clings unashamedly to the Creeley and the Bly, to the Gluck and the Tate, to the Hollander and the Hall, to the Olds and the Rich, as if they are rocks for the hand in a mad current of broken off images, encrusted bromides, burnt slabs of rhetoric, and jagged pieces of interrupted thought:

> LAMB
> | cuban
> | painter
>
> JASPER JOHNS—ANXIETY—A MAN WHO WANTED ME
> BUT I WAS
>   WRONG [4]
>   ....
> My collar holds a ball, mitts bulb-ended [5]
>
>   No wonder they call it Yaddo.
>   After Faber and Faber

it's the whitest, most minus-da-groove
diaperspace I go:

icka tit,
icka clit,
icka prick,
lickety-split.[6]
....
I dug you artless, I dug you out. Did you re-do?[7]
....
I'm John Fucking Keats returned in Kitty's body.[8]

Anyone would do as Hass did; hold on to the sound of a familiar
voice, to Yusef, to Ashbery, to Hillman, to Kizer and Koch. No matter
that it's the same old poetry club—or even your wife—no matter if the
poems are not some impossible-to-measure "best"—Hass knows he'll
be lucky to get out of Lehman's enterprise alive.

Just as we take the title of the book at face value, Hass takes his
responsibility as editor at face value. He does not know that the indefat-
igable Lehman, like a zany zen master, has posed to him an unsolvable
koan: *Grasshopper, what is the best American poetry for 2001?*

Every answer will be wrong. Meanwhile, Lehman seems to chortle
as he surfs America from his armchair, eager to document the next mis-
use of some lines of Shakespeare by a famous basketball player, some
star's revelation that he or she also writes poetry, a game show contes-
tant who can figure out the number of lines in a couplet. All evidence
that poets have a product America wants: "Readers do exist, more than
you might have thought. The trick remains how to reach them."

Here's a good trick Mr. Lehman: give us what you promise. Give us
a book full of poems that show mastery, that change us, that do for us
what poetry must do: make us feel something new, something deeper,
something that astonishes us and gives us pleasure; give us poems that
deliver the emotional and aesthetic and intellectual goods—that are,

without a doubt, the best. If your book is smaller by 50 percent, by 70 percent, by 90 percent, if you just give us one poem, but it is the best, then you will have done the job "that others have relinquished." If you cannot do this, then please change the name of this annual disappointment to *The Best I Can Do This Year*.

We'll understand.

NOTES:

1. *Nights,* Lyn Hejinian

2. *Doubt*, Fanny Howe

3. *Where Leftover Misery Goes*, Alice Notley

4. *Notes About My Face*, Michael Burkard

5. *Blouse of Felt*, Amina Calil

6. *T.A.P.O.A.F.O.M*, Thomas Sayers Elliss

7. *Music for Homemade Instruments*, Harryette Mullen

8. *Our Kitty*, Carole Muske Dukes

V. IF ONLY WE COULDN'T UNDERSTAND THEM

Because many contemporary poets have chosen the way of the mythical trickster, taking the reader through gullies and gorges thick with word-midge and image-mist (*Over here! No, over here!*) or into briar patches where the overlapping branches prickle with meaning just out of reach—and leaving us there—or tempting us with an apparent meaning of the poem, only to find that like touching a tar baby we are forever stuck onto it, our subsequent efforts to struggle free only making us more stuck; we are grateful, at least at first, for the Billy Collins poem.

As Billy Collins puts it:

"I think accessible just means that the reader can walk into the poem without difficulty. The poem is not, as someone put it, deflective of entry."[1]

Enter here. Enjoy the visit. Exit there.

"Often people, when they're confronted with a poem, it's like someone who keeps saying "what is the meaning of this? What is the meaning of this? And that dulls us to the other pleasures poetry offers." [2]

The other pleasures: all those pleasures aside from the one of discovering meaning in a poem. What are those other pleasures? Presumably, these are the elements of a poem—its imagery, metaphor, music, structure and so on. There's wordplay. Syntactical twists. Line breaks. Humor, perhaps. A storyline (but not one with a point—then it's fiction). Paradoxically, without the net, however fine, of meaning, to hold these elements together, to give them a shape and a raison d'être, the poem is much less accessible. Gertrude Stein, for example, meets all the criteria for "other pleasures" perfectly. So does much of John Ashbery. Without the hovering spirit of the author's shaping intellect and intentionality we are back in the briar patch. Enter anywhere. Wander around helplessly.

Exit nowhere.

On the other hand, the Billy Collins poem, though distinguished by its humor (an unusual, and welcome, attribute of contemporary poetry), has something major in common with a Mary Oliver poem, a Rita Dove poem, a David Lehman poem, and a Maya Angelou poem, among many other contemporary poets, because it is a poem we can understand. Immediately. We feel no drive to delve. It is not a poem we need to analyze. There are no pesky layers of meaning. What you see is what you get.

> "But the real question is what happens to the reader once he or she gets inside the poem." [3]

Mules of Love, a newly released book of poetry by Ellen Bass, is a book chock full of accessible poems. It is also a book lauded by, among other luminaries, Billy Collins:

> "The sudden intimacy of these poems of Ellen Bass will hold you to the page. She knows an awful lot and is ready to tell it all. her poems will quicken the pulse, and as you read you will become anxious to discover more and more, but she can only tell you so much, one good line at time, and that is more than enough."[4]

"...and that is more than enough." An ambiguous phrase, but one that points to Collins' previous statements about being satisfied with the "other pleasures" of a poem. If we suspend our need to find meaning, perhaps we will experience the "quickened pulse" the anxiety to "discover more and more" of what Collins found in Ms. Bass' book. For example, in the poem whose last line is used as the title of the book:

For My Daughter on Her Twenty-First Birthday

When they laid you in the crook
of my arms like a bouquet and I looked
into your eyes, dark bits of evening sky,
I thought, of course this is you,
like a person who has never seen the sea
can recognize it instantly.
They pulled you from me like a cork
and all the love flowed out. I adored you

> with the squandering passion of spring
> that shoots green from every pore.
>
> You dug me out like a well. You lit
> the deadwood of my heart. You pinned me
> to the earth with the points of stars.
>
> I was sure that kind of love would be
> enough. I thought I was your mother.
> How could I have known that over and over
> you would crack the sky like lightning,
> illuminating all my fears, my weaknesses, my sins.
>
> Massive the burden this flesh
> must learn to bear, like mules of love.

This is not only accessible, it's like walking into a Denny's restaurant. Familiar. Comfortable. Serving the same ol' stuff from the same ol' menu. With the meaning served first and out of the way, we look for the vaunted other pleasures of this poem. The fresh language, the surprising syntax and multi-level metaphor, the apt image.

> When they laid you in the crook
> of my arms like a bouquet...

Sweet. But no longer fresh.

> They pulled you from me like a cork
> and all the love flowed out...

Surprising but unintentionally comical (what is the sound of one baby popping?).

> You dug me out like a well. You lit
> the deadwood of my heart. You pinned me
> to the earth with the points of stars.

Is it too much to ask that the speaker be dug out like something other than a "well"? That she have a heart with something other than

109

"deadwood" in it to be "lit"? That she describe her love without using the words "earth" or "stars"?

> Massive the burden this flesh
> must learn to bear, like mules of love.

The final, resounding couplet. Problem: where is the referent for the simile "like mules of love?" What, exactly, is like "mules of love?" The burden? No, that can't be right. The burden is what the mules of love carry. So it must be an implied comparison between the mules of love and the act of learning to bear the massive burden; to wit: this burden I must bear (child and duty) is one I must learn to bear as mules of love do or would do if they were in my position; that is, having to carry something heavy (like duty) but with love. (He ain't heavy, he's my baby mule.)

"One good line at a time," Collins says. But if this be pleasure, in what does torture lie? Not only is the signature line in this poem racked with unintentional grammatical possibilities and irrelevancy of comparison (you have to wonder who selected it as the book's title), but the poem itself is full of amateurish gestures: overwriting, mixed metaphor, and trite language.

But—we can understand it. The problem is we don't want to. At least not so soon, not so easily, not without some kind of journey, some kind of new insight, something. Anything. We want more than gas and a handful of bromides for our trouble.

Ellen Bass writes of ordinary life with a fierce and loving passion. Her honesty, her insights, and her mastery of language, particularly metaphor, make this book compelling reading.[5]

Tempted by another goldplated blurb, we try again:

Tulip Blossoms
Tulip trees hang over the Kalihiwai River,
large lemon-yellow flowers dangling from both banks.
As my son and I glide in a rented kayak,

they fall to the celadon surface, floeating
like blessings in a private ritual.
When I smooth one open, the flat crepe petals
fan out, revealing a center so red
it's almost black—redder
than blood, or port,
or the deepest bing cherries—hidden
in the core of the blossom, the rippled base.
"It looks like an asshole,"
my son observes softly, almost
to himself. And I am glad,
remembering the first time
I saw his dusky asterisk,
its perfect creased rays—
glad he can see the flower
in the most humble, darkest star.

Mastery of language. Particularly metaphor. Redder than—of all things—blood! And port! And cherries! His "dusky asterisk"? Again, the "other pleasures" of this poem are chiefly absent—except for the son's one-liner, which provides some (unintentional) comic relief. There are no original, striking lines here (though the one-liner is at least memorable)—and, to cap it, it means something: the difficulty/joy of motherhood (albeit as described by a sentimental, rather amateurish writer). A meaning for which we didn't have to work (and, unfortunately, it's exactly worth all the work we did).

In some ways, such writing is worse than that which obfuscates and fancy-dances in order to create a dazzling surface, a distraction from its basic emptiness of content or intellect. The (too-obvious) meaning in a Bass poem cannot compensate for the lack of a dazzling surface. A poem without meaning is fine—as long as the poem does something with itself other than hanging around looking vacuous.

A paradoxical equation begins to emerge: perhaps the more accessible the poem, the fewer "other pleasures" the poem gives us. Meaning may be clear, but, as we see in Ms. Bass' poems, it may be meaning that's obvious or uninteresting. What is the purpose of accessibility if there is nothing interesting or new to access? Better to have a sound and fury signifying nothing, or not very much; a momentary play of language, something to admire in a line. Perhaps the sounds and syntactical twists, the sheer pyrotechnics of a Mary Jo Bang poem:

The Era

Of some reveller reeving through
the ringbolt of a mind,
merry wished and whistled now.

Pink promises fell like posies cranked robotic
from some well. Later he said, Look here,
earth is a low matter only, a pact
to grant and grovel for
parched by some latent bet
that was bound to go awry....

It may well be that the less meaning there is in the poem, the noisier it gets. Many Dylan Thomas poems prove this principle. A poem without meaning is fine—as long as the poem does something with itself other than hanging around looking vacuous. However, while the pleasure of language itself is better then diving into a poem and coming up with cliches, can't we expect poetry to give us both pleasure and meaning? This is the real difficulty, the challenge of poetry. Despite decades of talk therapy, even psychiatry has discovered that:

Despite the best efforts of poets, emotions are largely beyond words. [6]

In fact, it seems that the more difficult it is to express an emotional truth, or meaning if you will, the clearer, more accessible, more accurate, the language needs to be.

Franz Wright embodies this equation perfectly. The language of his poetry, never "tricky" or "dazzling" is in the service of a difficult quest for emotional truth and therefore needs to be absolutely clear, never distracting:

112

Thoughts of a Solitary Farmhouse

And not to feel bad about dying.
Not to take it so personally—

it is only
the force we exert all our lives

to exclude death from our thoughts
that confronts us, when it does arrive,

as the horror of being excluded— ...
something like that, the Canadian wind
coming in off Lake Erie
rattling the windows, horizontal snow

appearing out of nowhere
across the black highway and fields like billions of white bees.

Here, a plain-spoken narrator, in simple declarative sentences, makes an exact correlation between the articulated fear of death and its inarticulate power as reflected in the landscape. The brilliant hinge stanza, stanza four, leads us from a philosophical, "talking" meditation on death to a non-verbal fear of it, the words "something like that" casual in their expression of futility lead us to death's embodiment in natural imagery.

A brilliant and original language in the service of difficult emotional truth, by definition, renders the concept of accessibility null and void. For example, Dylan Thomas' handful of great poems exhibit meaning and all the other pleasures at once. This is also true of Hopkins and Stevens.

Sylvia Plath exemplifies the combination in most of her poems. In fact, it is this combination—original language in the service of difficult meaning—that is essential for greatness in poetry.

Contrary to Collins' remarks then, it may be that the other pleasures of poetry arise from difficulty itself. If a poem is to be more than entertainment, if, in fact, it is to be great, then it must express difficult truth, both originally and clearly. The challenge for a poet is to put those other pleasures in the service of meaning.

The following sources are cited in this article:

1, 2, and 3. Billy Collins, in an interview with Elizabeth Farnsworth on *NewsHour with Jim Lehrer*
4. Billy Collins, blurb from *Mules of Love*, BOA Editions, 2001
5. Linda Pastan, blurb from *Mules of Love*, BOA Editions, 2001
6. Jerome Kagan quoted in "Why Psychiatry has Failed" by Peter Watson.

The following poems are cited in this article:

For My Daughter on Her Twenty-First Birthday by Ellen Bass
Tulip Blossoms by Ellen Bass
The Era, stanzas 1-3, by Mary Jo Bang
Thoughts of a Solitary Farmhouse by Franz Wright

About the Author

Joan Houlihan is editor of *Perihelion*, a magazine that focuses on contemporary poetry, reviews, translations and interviews, and is published at *webdelsol.com*, the nation's largest publisher of contemporary periodical literature. Her column on contemporary American poetry, *The Boston Comment*, also appears on this site, as well as on *Arts and Letters Daily*. She is the author of *Our New and Smaller Lives*, a chapbook collection published by Black Warrior Review. She lives with her husband and twin sons in Acton, Massachusetts.

Printed in the United States
1026700004B

9 780615 123110